Should You Be
Laughing at This?

Hugleikur Dagsson

Should You Be Laughing at This?

MICHAEL JOSEPH
an imprint of
PENGUIN BOOKS

MICHAEL JOSEPH

Published by the Penguin Group
Penguin Books Ltd, 80 Strand, London WC2R ORL, England
Penguin Group (USA) Inc., 375 Hudson Street, New York, New York 10014, USA
Penguin Group (Canada), 90 Eglinton Avenue East, Suite 700, Toronto, Ontario, Canada M4P 2Y3
(a division of Pearson Penguin Canada Inc.)
Penguin Ireland, 25 St Stephen's Green, Dublin 2, Ireland (a division of Penguin Books Ltd)
Penguin Group (Australia), 250 Camberwell Road,
Camberwell, Victoria 3124, Australia (a division of Pearson Australia Group Pty Ltd)
Penguin Books India Pvt Ltd, 11 Community Centre,
Penguin Group (NZ), 67 Apollo Drive, Mairangi Bay, Auckland 1310, New Zealand
(a division of Pearson New Zealand Ltd)
Penguin Books (South Africa) (Pty) Ltd, 24 Sturdee Avenue,
Rosebank, Johannesburg 2196, South Africa

Penguin Books Ltd, Registered Offices: 80 Strand, London WC2R ORL, England

www.penguin.com

First published as *Avoid Us* by JPV Publishers, Iceland 2006
Published by Michael Joseph 2006
1

Copyright © Hugleikur Dagsson, 2006

The moral right of the author has been asserted

Printed in Great Britain by Clays Ltd, St Ives plc

A CIP catalogue record for this book is available from the British Library

ISBN-13: 978-0-718-15220-8
ISBN-10: 0-718-15220-4

Prologue

Finally this book has been made available for the non-Icelandic reader. In Iceland it is a famous good book. It contains the bulk of three small books originally published separately for greater profit. Books have been written in Iceland for more than eighty years and in Iceland, reading them is our favourite pastime. The harsh climate becomes soft and cozy when you read a book.

Hugleikur's books have been a huge success in Iceland, and why shouldn't they be "the talk of the town" elsewhere as well? If there ever were a capturer of moments such as our Hully, a wanderer better equipped, a prophesy sung in higher notes; let that selfsame know that he is a true warrior. The success of Hully's books in Iceland spawned a theatrical outcry of his rage when in October 2005 a play was premiered starring some of Iceland's most prominent acting students. They took to the stage and did their very best. Hully has been „the talk of the town" ever since.

I am in love with a demon. Hully has through his simple artwork built a bridge between the educated artist's outlets and the pretty public. A bridge over troubled water. The masses in Iceland have taken to Hully's books like mice to cheese and the educated artist is by no means less enthralled.

Hully's humour may be local but on the other hand it may also be universal. Only time will tell.

Fridrik Solnes, electrician.

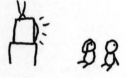

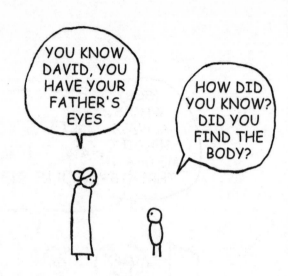

IF YOU CAN'T EVEN MAKE IT ACROSS THE STREET ON YOUR OWN, THEN WHY THE FUCK DID YOU EVEN LEAVE THE FUCKING HOUSE IN THE FIRST PLACE, BITCH??!!!!

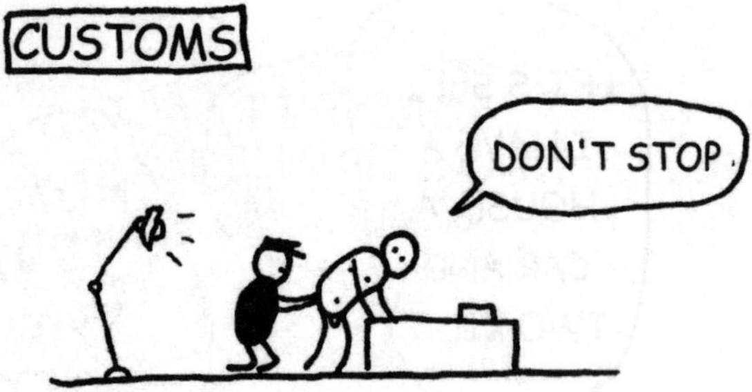
CUSTOMS
DON'T STOP.

HMM... WHO SHALL WE BULLY THIS SEMESTER?

YES. WHO INDEED.

SORRY I'M LATE SWEETY. I HOPE YOU MANAGED TO FIX YOUR DINNER BY YOURSELF.
I ATE A RAT.

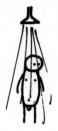

ONE FOR BRIDGET JONES.

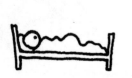

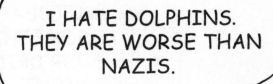

BleEUGHH!